THE SIMPLE GRATITUDE JOURNAL

A NOTEBOOK FOR MEN & TEEN BOYS

Don't forget to grab your bonus freebies today!

WWW.123JOURNALIT.COM / FREEBIES

SCRIPTURE FLASHCARDS - BIBLE READING PROMPTS - JOURNALING PAGES

More information at: www.123journalit.com

First Printing: May 2018
1 2 3 Journal It Publishing

ISBN-13: 978-1-947209-49-7
Pocketbook 6x9-in. Format Size
From the *Christian Workbooks* Series

THIS JOURNAL BELONGS TO

_____

WHAT I AM THANKFUL FOR THE WEEK OF _____ TO _____

MONDAY:

TUESDAY:

WEDNESDAY:

THURSDAY:

FRIDAY:

SATURDAY:

SUNDAY:

MY NOTES & INSPIRATIONAL QUOTES:

_____

_____

_____

_____

_____

WHAT I AM THANKFUL FOR THE WEEK OF _____ TO _____

MONDAY:

TUESDAY:

WEDNESDAY:

THURSDAY:

FRIDAY:

SATURDAY:

SUNDAY:

MY NOTES & INSPIRATIONAL QUOTES:

WHAT I AM THANKFUL FOR THE WEEK OF _____ TO _____

MONDAY:

TUESDAY:

WEDNESDAY:

THURSDAY:

FRIDAY:

SATURDAY:

SUNDAY:

MY NOTES & INSPIRATIONAL QUOTES:

WHAT I AM THANKFUL FOR THE WEEK OF _____ TO _____

MONDAY:

TUESDAY:

WEDNESDAY:

THURSDAY:

FRIDAY:

SATURDAY:

SUNDAY:

MY NOTES & INSPIRATIONAL QUOTES:

WHAT I AM THANKFUL FOR THE WEEK OF _____ TO _____

MONDAY:

TUESDAY:

WEDNESDAY:

THURSDAY:

FRIDAY:

SATURDAY:

SUNDAY:

MY NOTES & INSPIRATIONAL QUOTES:

_____

_____

_____

_____

_____

_____

WHAT I AM THANKFUL FOR THE WEEK OF _____ TO _____

MONDAY:

TUESDAY:

WEDNESDAY:

THURSDAY:

FRIDAY:

SATURDAY:

SUNDAY:

MY NOTES & INSPIRATIONAL QUOTES:

_____
_____
_____
_____
_____

WHAT I AM THANKFUL FOR THE WEEK OF _____ TO _____

MONDAY:

TUESDAY:

WEDNESDAY:

THURSDAY:

FRIDAY:

SATURDAY:

SUNDAY:

MY NOTES & INSPIRATIONAL QUOTES:

WHAT I AM THANKFUL FOR THE WEEK OF _____ TO _____

MONDAY:

TUESDAY:

WEDNESDAY:

THURSDAY:

FRIDAY:

SATURDAY:

SUNDAY:

MY NOTES & INSPIRATIONAL QUOTES:

WHAT I AM THANKFUL FOR THE WEEK OF _____ TO _____

MONDAY:

TUESDAY:

WEDNESDAY:

THURSDAY:

FRIDAY:

SATURDAY:

SUNDAY:

MY NOTES & INSPIRATIONAL QUOTES:

WHAT I AM THANKFUL FOR THE WEEK OF _____ TO _____

MONDAY:

TUESDAY:

WEDNESDAY:

THURSDAY:

FRIDAY:

SATURDAY:

SUNDAY:

MY NOTES & INSPIRATIONAL QUOTES:

WHAT I AM THANKFUL FOR THE WEEK OF _____ TO _____

MONDAY:

TUESDAY:

WEDNESDAY:

THURSDAY:

FRIDAY:

SATURDAY:

SUNDAY:

MY NOTES & INSPIRATIONAL QUOTES:

WHAT I AM THANKFUL FOR THE WEEK OF _____ TO _____

MONDAY:

TUESDAY:

WEDNESDAY:

THURSDAY:

FRIDAY:

SATURDAY:

SUNDAY:

MY NOTES & INSPIRATIONAL QUOTES:

WHAT I AM THANKFUL FOR THE WEEK OF _____ TO _____

MONDAY:

TUESDAY:

WEDNESDAY:

THURSDAY:

FRIDAY:

SATURDAY:

SUNDAY:

MY NOTES & INSPIRATIONAL QUOTES:

WHAT I AM THANKFUL FOR THE WEEK OF _____ TO _____

MONDAY:

TUESDAY:

WEDNESDAY:

THURSDAY:

FRIDAY:

SATURDAY:

SUNDAY:

MY NOTES & INSPIRATIONAL QUOTES:

WHAT I AM THANKFUL FOR THE WEEK OF _____ TO _____

MONDAY:

TUESDAY:

WEDNESDAY:

THURSDAY:

FRIDAY:

SATURDAY:

SUNDAY:

MY NOTES & INSPIRATIONAL QUOTES:

WHAT I AM THANKFUL FOR THE WEEK OF _____ TO _____

MONDAY:

TUESDAY:

WEDNESDAY:

THURSDAY:

FRIDAY:

- -
- -
- -
- -

SATURDAY:

- -
- -
- -
- -

SUNDAY:

- -
- -
- -
- -

MY NOTES & INSPIRATIONAL QUOTES:

WHAT I AM THANKFUL FOR THE WEEK OF _____ TO _____

MONDAY:

TUESDAY:

WEDNESDAY:

THURSDAY:

FRIDAY:

SATURDAY:

SUNDAY:

MY NOTES & INSPIRATIONAL QUOTES:

_____
_____
_____
_____
_____
_____

WHAT I AM THANKFUL FOR THE WEEK OF _____ TO _____

MONDAY:

TUESDAY:

WEDNESDAY:

THURSDAY:

FRIDAY:

SATURDAY:

SUNDAY:

MY NOTES & INSPIRATIONAL QUOTES:

WHAT I AM THANKFUL FOR THE WEEK OF _____ TO _____

MONDAY:

TUESDAY:

WEDNESDAY:

THURSDAY:

FRIDAY:

SATURDAY:

SUNDAY:

MY NOTES & INSPIRATIONAL QUOTES:

_____

_____

_____

_____

_____

_____

WHAT I AM THANKFUL FOR THE WEEK OF _____ TO _____

MONDAY:

TUESDAY:

WEDNESDAY:

THURSDAY:

FRIDAY:

SATURDAY:

SUNDAY:

MY NOTES & INSPIRATIONAL QUOTES:

WHAT I AM THANKFUL FOR THE WEEK OF _____ TO _____

MONDAY:

TUESDAY:

WEDNESDAY:

THURSDAY:

FRIDAY:

SATURDAY:

SUNDAY:

MY NOTES & INSPIRATIONAL QUOTES:

_____

_____

_____

_____

_____

WHAT I AM THANKFUL FOR THE WEEK OF _____ TO _____

MONDAY:

TUESDAY:

WEDNESDAY:

THURSDAY:

FRIDAY:

SATURDAY:

SUNDAY:

MY NOTES & INSPIRATIONAL QUOTES:

WHAT I AM THANKFUL FOR THE WEEK OF _____ TO _____

MONDAY:

TUESDAY:

WEDNESDAY:

THURSDAY:

FRIDAY:

SATURDAY:

SUNDAY:

MY NOTES & INSPIRATIONAL QUOTES:

WHAT I AM THANKFUL FOR THE WEEK OF _____TO_____

MONDAY:

TUESDAY:

WEDNESDAY:

THURSDAY:

FRIDAY:

SATURDAY:

SUNDAY:

MY NOTES & INSPIRATIONAL QUOTES:

WHAT I AM THANKFUL FOR THE WEEK OF _____ TO _____

MONDAY:

TUESDAY:

WEDNESDAY:

THURSDAY:

FRIDAY:

SATURDAY:

SUNDAY:

MY NOTES & INSPIRATIONAL QUOTES:

WHAT I AM THANKFUL FOR THE WEEK OF _____ TO _____

MONDAY:

TUESDAY:

WEDNESDAY:

THURSDAY:

FRIDAY:

SATURDAY:

SUNDAY:

MY NOTES & INSPIRATIONAL QUOTES:

WHAT I AM THANKFUL FOR THE WEEK OF _____ TO _____

MONDAY:

TUESDAY:

WEDNESDAY:

THURSDAY:

FRIDAY:

SATURDAY:

SUNDAY:

MY NOTES & INSPIRATIONAL QUOTES:

WHAT I AM THANKFUL FOR THE WEEK OF _____ TO _____

MONDAY:

TUESDAY:

WEDNESDAY:

THURSDAY:

FRIDAY:

SATURDAY:

SUNDAY:

MY NOTES & INSPIRATIONAL QUOTES:

WHAT I AM THANKFUL FOR THE WEEK OF _____ TO _____

MONDAY:

TUESDAY:

WEDNESDAY:

THURSDAY:

FRIDAY:

SATURDAY:

SUNDAY:

MY NOTES & INSPIRATIONAL QUOTES:

WHAT I AM THANKFUL FOR THE WEEK OF _____ TO _____

MONDAY:

_____

_____

_____

_____

TUESDAY:

_____

_____

_____

_____

WEDNESDAY:

_____

_____

_____

_____

THURSDAY:

_____

_____

_____

_____

FRIDAY:

SATURDAY:

SUNDAY:

MY NOTES & INSPIRATIONAL QUOTES:

WHAT I AM THANKFUL FOR THE WEEK OF _____ TO _____

MONDAY:

TUESDAY:

WEDNESDAY:

THURSDAY:

FRIDAY:

SATURDAY:

SUNDAY:

MY NOTES & INSPIRATIONAL QUOTES:

WHAT I AM THANKFUL FOR THE WEEK OF _____ TO _____

MONDAY:

TUESDAY:

WEDNESDAY:

THURSDAY:

FRIDAY:

SATURDAY:

SUNDAY:

MY NOTES & INSPIRATIONAL QUOTES:

WHAT I AM THANKFUL FOR THE WEEK OF _____ TO _____

MONDAY:

TUESDAY:

WEDNESDAY:

THURSDAY:

FRIDAY:

SATURDAY:

SUNDAY:

MY NOTES & INSPIRATIONAL QUOTES:

WHAT I AM THANKFUL FOR THE WEEK OF _____ TO _____

MONDAY:

TUESDAY:

WEDNESDAY:

THURSDAY:

FRIDAY:

SATURDAY:

SUNDAY:

MY NOTES & INSPIRATIONAL QUOTES:

WHAT I AM THANKFUL FOR THE WEEK OF _____ TO _____

MONDAY:

TUESDAY:

WEDNESDAY:

THURSDAY:

FRIDAY:

SATURDAY:

SUNDAY:

MY NOTES & INSPIRATIONAL QUOTES:

WHAT I AM THANKFUL FOR THE WEEK OF _____ TO _____

MONDAY:

TUESDAY:

WEDNESDAY:

THURSDAY:

FRIDAY:

SATURDAY:

SUNDAY:

MY NOTES & INSPIRATIONAL QUOTES:

_____

_____

_____

_____

_____

WHAT I AM THANKFUL FOR THE WEEK OF _____TO _____

MONDAY:

TUESDAY:

WEDNESDAY:

THURSDAY:

FRIDAY:

SATURDAY:

SUNDAY:

MY NOTES & INSPIRATIONAL QUOTES:

WHAT I AM THANKFUL FOR THE WEEK OF _____ TO _____

MONDAY:

TUESDAY:

WEDNESDAY:

THURSDAY:

FRIDAY:

SATURDAY:

SUNDAY:

MY NOTES & INSPIRATIONAL QUOTES:

WHAT I AM THANKFUL FOR THE WEEK OF _____ TO _____

MONDAY:

TUESDAY:

WEDNESDAY:

THURSDAY:

FRIDAY:

SATURDAY:

SUNDAY:

MY NOTES & INSPIRATIONAL QUOTES:

WHAT I AM THANKFUL FOR THE WEEK OF _____ TO _____

MONDAY:

TUESDAY:

WEDNESDAY:

THURSDAY:

FRIDAY:

SATURDAY:

SUNDAY:

MY NOTES & INSPIRATIONAL QUOTES:

WHAT I AM THANKFUL FOR THE WEEK OF _____ TO _____

MONDAY:

TUESDAY:

WEDNESDAY:

THURSDAY:

FRIDAY:

SATURDAY:

SUNDAY:

MY NOTES & INSPIRATIONAL QUOTES:

WHAT I AM THANKFUL FOR THE WEEK OF _____ TO _____

MONDAY:

TUESDAY:

WEDNESDAY:

THURSDAY:

FRIDAY:

SATURDAY:

SUNDAY:

MY NOTES & INSPIRATIONAL QUOTES:

_____
_____
_____
_____
_____
_____

WHAT I AM THANKFUL FOR THE WEEK OF _____ TO _____

MONDAY:

TUESDAY:

WEDNESDAY:

THURSDAY:

FRIDAY:

SATURDAY:

SUNDAY:

MY NOTES & INSPIRATIONAL QUOTES:

WHAT I AM THANKFUL FOR THE WEEK OF _____ TO _____

MONDAY:

TUESDAY:

WEDNESDAY:

THURSDAY:

FRIDAY:

SATURDAY:

SUNDAY:

MY NOTES & INSPIRATIONAL QUOTES:

WHAT I AM THANKFUL FOR THE WEEK OF _____ TO _____

MONDAY:

TUESDAY:

WEDNESDAY:

THURSDAY:

FRIDAY:

SATURDAY:

SUNDAY:

MY NOTES & INSPIRATIONAL QUOTES:

WHAT I AM THANKFUL FOR THE WEEK OF _____ TO _____

MONDAY:

TUESDAY:

WEDNESDAY:

THURSDAY:

FRIDAY:

SATURDAY:

SUNDAY:

MY NOTES & INSPIRATIONAL QUOTES:

WHAT I AM THANKFUL FOR THE WEEK OF _____ TO _____

MONDAY:

TUESDAY:

WEDNESDAY:

THURSDAY:

FRIDAY:

SATURDAY:

SUNDAY:

MY NOTES & INSPIRATIONAL QUOTES:

_____

_____

_____

_____

_____

WHAT I AM THANKFUL FOR THE WEEK OF _____ TO _____

MONDAY:

TUESDAY:

WEDNESDAY:

THURSDAY:

FRIDAY:

SATURDAY:

SUNDAY:

MY NOTES & INSPIRATIONAL QUOTES:

WHAT I AM THANKFUL FOR THE WEEK OF _____ TO _____

MONDAY:

TUESDAY:

WEDNESDAY:

THURSDAY:

FRIDAY:

SATURDAY:

SUNDAY:

MY NOTES & INSPIRATIONAL QUOTES:

WHAT I AM THANKFUL FOR THE WEEK OF _____ TO _____

MONDAY:

TUESDAY:

WEDNESDAY:

THURSDAY:

FRIDAY:

SATURDAY:

SUNDAY:

MY NOTES & INSPIRATIONAL QUOTES:

WHAT I AM THANKFUL FOR THE WEEK OF _____ TO _____

MONDAY:

TUESDAY:

WEDNESDAY:

THURSDAY:

FRIDAY:

SATURDAY:

SUNDAY:

MY NOTES & INSPIRATIONAL QUOTES:

_____
_____
_____
_____
_____

WHAT I AM THANKFUL FOR THE WEEK OF _____ TO _____

MONDAY:

TUESDAY:

WEDNESDAY:

THURSDAY:

FRIDAY:

SATURDAY:

SUNDAY:

MY NOTES & INSPIRATIONAL QUOTES:

20012415R00068

Made in the USA
Lexington, KY
01 December 2018